D1307788

Governor Arnold

A Photodiary of His First 100 Days in Office

Andy Borowitz

SIMON & SCHUSTER

NEW YORK   LONDON   TORONTO   SYDNEY

SIMON & SCHUSTER
Rockefeller Center
1230 Avenue of the Americas
New York, NY 10020

First Simon & Schuster trade paperback edition 2004

For information regarding special discounts for bulk purchases, please contact Simon & Schuster Special Sales at 1-800-456-6798 or business@simonandschuster.com.

Designed by Charles Kreloff

Manufactured in the United States of America

10   9   8   7   6   5   4   3   2   1

Library of Congress Cataloging-in-Publication Data is available.

ISBN 0-7432-6266-2

"I like the noise of democracy."

—James Buchanan (1791–1868),
fifteenth U.S president

"ARRRGGGGHHHH!"

—California Governor Arnold Schwarzenegger,
in *Pumping Iron* (1977)

On the night of October 7, 2003, California's governor-elect Arnold Schwarzenegger delivered a rousing victory speech in the ballroom of Los Angeles's Century Plaza Hotel, flanked onstage by friends, supporters, and a woman most people assumed to be his wife, Maria Shriver—but who was, in actuality, me.

Hours earlier, a team of top makeup artists had undertaken the challenge of transforming me into a dead ringer for Ms. Shriver, installing prosthetic cheekbones and filling my mouth with an additional twenty-seven teeth. As I slipped into my Donna Karan cocktail dress, even I had to admit that I looked pretty damn hot. But there was no time to linger at the mirror, taking in the gorgeous view. I was a photojournalist, and I had a job to do.

Minutes later I was onstage, surreptitiously snapping photos of California's new governor, who seemed totally unaware that the strapping six-foot-five man beside him was not his wife. As he cooed into my ear,

"Maria, you have got it going on tonight," playfully grabbing my right buttock with his kung-fu grip, I comforted myself with the knowledge that the legendary photographer Matthew Brady probably endured similar indignities at the hands of Abraham Lincoln, if not worse. When Ms. Shriver finally chewed through her bonds and tore into the ballroom screaming like a banshee, I bolted as fast as my Manolo Blahnik slingbacks would allow—but my work, by then, was done.

Thus began my career as the chronicler of Governor Schwarzenegger's administration, the first hundred days of which this book attempts to capture in all its vivid pageantry: the tough decisions, the legislative battles, the photo opportunities involving silly hats. The photos in this book, of course, cannot tell the whole story of Governor Arnold's term in office since that story is still very much being written. If you'll permit me to coin a phrase: I'll be back.

Governor Arnold

In his first day in office, Governor Schwarzenegger and his chief of staff differ about the precise location of Sacramento.

Governor Schwarzenegger tackles the first difficult decision of his term in office.

Doing some housecleaning at the governor's mansion, Governor Schwarzenegger throws out a big wooden stick believed to have been lodged inside former Governor Gray Davis during his entire time in office.

Governor Schwarzenegger bids farewell to a final holdover from Governor Davis's staff.

In his first appearance before the legislature, Governor Schwarzenegger lays out his vision of bipartisan cooperation.

After a contentious meeting in Sacramento, Governor Schwarzenegger holds up what is left of the Democratic leader of the Assembly.

Governor Schwarzenegger's aides applaud his decision to introduce casual Fridays to Sacramento.

Governor Schwarzenegger vows to have a good working relationship with a former political rival, Lieutenant Governor Cruz Bustamante.

Governor Schwarzenegger describes a cordial meeting with former gubernatorial rival Gary Coleman.

Governor Schwarzenegger implores former rival Arianna Huffington to retrieve a personal item she left behind at one of the gubernatorial debates.

Governor Schwarzenegger emerges from his first meeting on the state's budget shortfalls.

In a bid to boost tourism, Governor Schwarzenegger declares January 8 "Tiny Shiny Thong Day."

Governor Schwarzenegger's gift for stagecraft is very much in evidence in his first official press conference at the governor's mansion.

Governor Schwarzenegger attempts to travel back in time to locate California's budget surplus.

Working into the wee hours with a member of his gubernatorial staff, Governor Schwarzenegger gropes for solutions to California's toughest problems.

Governor Schwarzenegger realizes that he is late for an appearance on *The Tonight Show with Jay Leno*.

After Governor Schwarzenegger asks President George W. Bush for a massive financial-aid package for California, the President refuses to look the Governor in the eye for the rest of their four-hour meeting.

In a visit to the Smithsonian Institution in Washington, Governor Schwarzenegger poses between sculptures of two famous Americans.

In a closed-door session with prominent Republican donors, Governor Schwarzenegger warns that he will not be held hostage by special interest groups.

Governor Schwarzenegger announces that his number one legislative priority will be naming the Macarena the official state dance.

Vowing "never to forget where I came from," Governor Schwarzenegger takes a break from his busy schedule to kiss his collection of movie awards.

Governor Schwarzenegger uses a photo opportunity in Fresno to appeal simultaneously to two constituencies: the National Rifle Association and the gay community.

At the California State Fair in Calabasas, Governor Schwarzenegger remarks that pretending to play the guitar is "a cinch" compared to pretending to govern the state.

In a show of respect to his predecessor, Governor Schwarzenegger pays a visit to the newly opened Gray Davis Library in Costa Mesa.

An exultant Governor Schwarzenegger tells the people of California that he just got a lower rate on his auto insurance from Geico.

A man of his word, Governor Schwarzenegger prepares to drive through a loophole in Arianna Huffington's tax return.

In keeping with his image as a "big tent" Republican, Governor Schwarzenegger welcomes a representative from the National Organization for Women (NOW).

Governor Schwarzenegger visits a mall in San Francisco to encourage Californians to go Christmas shopping, accompanied by former Hollywood superagent Michael Ovitz.

Governor Schwarzenegger silences a heckler during the traditional State of the State Address.

Governor Schwarzenegger attempts to single-handedly repair California's beleaguered electrical grid.

Governor Schwarzenegger proposes a new law-enforcement tool to stem the flow of illegal aliens.

In an effort to appease the gun-control lobby, Governor Schwarzenegger proposes a two-week waiting period on the purchase of all toy assault rifles.

The governor is mistakenly jailed for a night after a man resembling him is seen fondling women and praising Hitler on a movie set.

Governor Schwarzenegger makes history once more, becoming the first California governor to turn his routine physical exam into a live pay-per-view event.

The governor suffers a minor setback after the governor of Nevada hustles him for California's fiscal 2004 tax revenues.

A new poll shows that two out of three California voters are pleased with Governor Schwarzenegger's job performance.

Governor Schwarzenegger makes good on a campaign promise to look down the dress of every mother in California.

Governor Schwarzenegger presides over the dedication of a bust of former Governor Gray Davis.

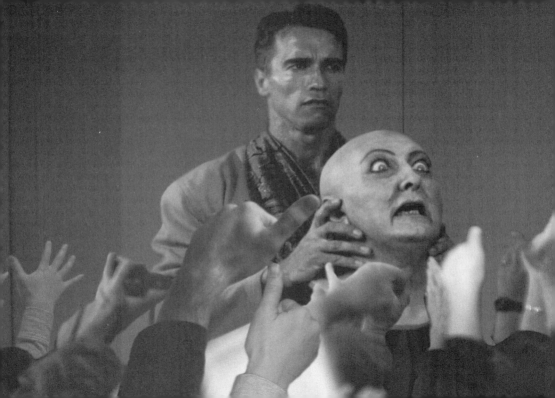

In Sacramento, Governor Schwarzenegger shows off a new ring-sized power cell that enables him to function for up to six hours without recharging.

Governor Schwarzenegger places a temporary freeze on his and his wife's facial expressions.

Governor Schwarzenegger vigorously denies Democratic allegations that he has become drunk with power.

Governor Schwarzenegger breaks with tradition, renaming the official governor's aircraft "The Mile-High Club Express."

Governor Schwarzenegger disciplines his head speechwriter for failing to include the lines "I'll be back" or "Hasta la vista, baby" in the governor's latest speech.

Governor Schwarzenegger authorizes releasing California's strategic Botox reserves.

Governor Schwarzenegger launches a fact-finding mission to determine why the metal detectors in the Capitol building keep going off.

Governor Schwarzenegger acknowledges that his controversial proposal to breed a "Californian Master Race" faces an uphill fight in the legislature.

Calling them "a scourge on California's workplace productivity," Governor Schwarzenegger spends seventy-two hours studying Internet porn sites.

Governor Schwarzenegger poses with well-wishers at a
Republican picnic in Pasadena.

The 2005 state budget is presented to Governor Schwarzenegger in a new, easy-to-read format.

Governor Schwarzenegger shares a light moment with mother-in-law Eunice Kennedy Shriver.

Governor Schwarzenegger announces the release of the Special Golden Edition DVD of his first hundred days in office, including narration by the governor and never-before-seen footage.

Andy Borowitz is a writer and performer whose humor appears in *The New Yorker*, *The New York Times*, and at *Newsweek.com*. He is the author of *Who Moved My Soap?: The CEO's Guide to Surviving in Prison*. He is an essayist on National Public Radio's *Weekend Edition Sunday*, a contributor to CNN's *American Morning*, and the creator of the award-winning humor site www.borowitzreport.com.

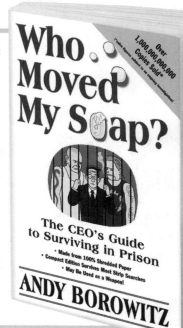